# The Power of Praise

# A study from scripture

## Pastor James Carley

# Foreword

It is a great honour to write the foreword for this book on the importance of praise, written by my father. This book is above all written from a "lived experience" and so comes with a force of truth that goes beyond mere words. The book while a blessing for all will I believe be a comfort especially to those who are going through times of difficulty, sadness or sickness.

My dad has had his fair share of all of these.

Dad was born into a rural home, a child of his mother's second marriage. Having been widowed as a young woman, she had converted to Roman Catholicism to marry my grandfather. My dad therefore grew up in a Catholic home but had older siblings who remained protestant. At the age of 16 my father, in an attempt to get closer to where my mother lived, joined the Irish Army only to find himself further away, but that's a whole other story. As a young couple, both aged 18 they were soundly saved under the ministry of Stuart Snoxell, an Assemblies of God Pioneer at an "open air" meeting in Dublin city.

And so, I had the blessing of being born into believing

home, where prayer and praise, and the Pentecostal gifts were the norm. One of my early memories is of dad returning from a meeting and teaching my brother and sister and I the latest chorus which was "Surely Goodness and mercy, shall follow me, all the days of my life". And so it has.

As a family we were constantly reminded of Romans 8:28, "all things work together for good". I must confess that at times for me it was just words, but on the night my dad had his first heart attack some 34 years ago, the first thing he said as I stood to pray with him in hospital, was just that Romans 8:28. Since then dad has had all sorts of heart surgeries but has never wavered from that stance. More recently in November 2016 following a minor surgery my dad suffered a severe stroke. This was a very dark moment. A preacher and teacher he had lost his voice. The entry in my devotional diary simply says "Lord give dad back his voice. He has honoured You with his lips, don't put him in silence at this age". The following day, my dad uttered his first word. Finding himself unable to speak, his whole vocabulary lost, he had begun to "speak in tongues", sensibly doing it silently in his mind, he said he knew if he began to speak audibly it would have caused undue concern. During the night he began to recite the Lord's prayer, one word coming after the other, he then moved to Psalm 23, until the following day he was able to begin to communicate. Today 2021 he writes a daily devotional on Facebook.

Remarkably the contents of this small book were written just after Easter 2017 , April of that year, so it comes only six months after his stroke. He suffered no long term effects from his stroke.

And so I commend this book for the fact, that it was forged not on the hilltop but in the valley.

Pastor Paul R Carley

## Introduction.

It was on the Sunday before Easter 2017, during our Church service as we were worshipping together that I became deeply aware that something special, something heavenly was happening. As we worshipped I became aware that the Holy Spirit was moving also in the gift of prophecy.

At that service I decided to look into the Power of Praise, and this booklet is a result of that endeavor.

May it be a blessing to all who read it.

Jim

# The Power of Praise

## Ephesians 1:3-6   (NASB)

*"Blessed be God and Father of our Lord Jesus Christ, who has blessed us with every spiritual blessing in the heavenly places in Christ, just as He chose us in Him before the foundation of the world, that we should be holy and blameless before Him in love. He predestined us to adoption as sons through Jesus Christ to Himself , according to the kind intention of His will, to the praise and glory of His grace, which He freely bestowed on us His beloved."*

A suitable format for a hymn of praise is found in *Isaiah*

12

*then you shall say on that day,*

*"I will give thanks to the Lord; for although Thou wast angry with me,*

*Thine anger is turned away And Thou dost comfort me"*

*Behold God is my salvation, I will trust and not be afraid*

*For the Lord God is my strength and song,*

*And He has become my salvation.*

*Therefore you will joyously draw water, from the springs of salvation.*

*And in that day you will say,*

*"Give thanks to the Lord, call on His name, make known His deeds among the people*

*Make then to remember that His name is exalted.*

*Praise the Lord in song, for He has done excellent things*

*Let this be known throughout the earth.*

*Cry aloud and shout for joy, o inhabitant of Zion*

*For great in your midst is the Holy One of Israel.*

Praise, in Greek *Epainos (ep-ahee-nos).* *Approbation, commendation, approval, praise.*

Epainos, expresses not only praise for what God does for us, but also for whom He is, recognizing His glory. ***Psalm 50:23 "whoever offers praise, Glorifies Me".*** In our initial text of ***Ephesians 1:5-6*** , we read that we were predestined to adoption as sons, through Jesus Christ according to the will of the Father, " ***To the praise of the glory of His grace"*** and are fully accepted in ***"the Beloved"***, that is Jesus.

Our lives then are lived to the praise of His glory, as grace abounds in us, transforming us into the image of His son.

In ***Psalm 100:4*** we read ***"enter His gates with thanksgiving and into His courts with praise. Be thankful and bless His name"***

The word translated here as praise is ***Tehillah (Plural Tehillim)***, a hymn of praise celebrating someone or something worthy, a lauding of or exaltation of God, a song of admiration for the acts done.

The word "Tehillah" comes from the noun Halal, which

7

means praise celebrate or laud. The Hebrew title for the Book of Psalms is Tehillim or literally *"The Book of Praise"*. It is from the same word that we get *Hallelujah.*

*Psalm 22-3* describes God as being *"enthroned in the praises of Israel"* and since God is thus enthroned in the praises of His people, worship is the key to entering fully into His presence. The concept here is that praise releases God's glory thus bringing to the worshippers actualized responses to His kingly reign. His kingly responses through the operation of the Holy Spirit or manifestations of the Holy Spirit can be prophecy, healings, miracles, a call to reverential silence, conviction of sin, or salvation of sinners.

This key verse of scripture should be our guiding source for personal and corporate worship. Praise will bring us into the presence of God, although God is in fact everywhere, as we draw close in worship there is a distinct and tangible manifestation which enters into an environment of praise.

Here we have the remedy for times when one feels alone, deserted or depressed. Praise however simple your song as a testimony of God's goodness in your life, expresses the Glory of God and the result will be that God enters into your situation and His presence will take residence in your life.

The Hebrew *Yashab can* be translated as inhabit, so *Psalm 22:3* can also be stated as

*"God inhabits the praises of Israel".* Yashab then is to sit down, to remain, to settle and even to marry. In other words God does not merely visit us when we praise but His presence abides with us and we are partners with Him in an ever deepening relationship. *Psalm 22* that God dwells in the praise of His people goes on to speak of Trust and Deliverance, and enduring faithfulness, verse 5, says

*"In Thee they trusted and were not disappointed".*

Whatever our situation or problem God will not be a disappointment to us, as we enter into His courts with praise; we find great deliverance and uplifting of our head.

*Psalm 18 :3 "I will call upon the Lord, who is worthy to be praised, and I am saved from my enemies".*

Our most basic reason for praising God is that He is worthy of our praise, always and whatever the circumstances we face, He is worthy. In its most primitive meaning the Hebrew word *Halal* means "to cause to shine" or "to show", so as we praise God we turn as it were the spotlight on our God who is worthy and deserves to be praised, and is willing and able to deliver us, and in doing so turn away from ourselves and that which afflicts us. As we are a reflection of Him the more we focus our worship on Him the more we reflect His glory and shine.

*Psalm 7: 14-17*

*"behold the wicked brings forth iniquity, he conceives trouble and brings forth falsehood. He made a pit and dug it out and has fallen into the ditch which he made. His trouble shall return on his own head and his violent dealings shall come down on his crown. I will praise the Lord according to His righteousness and I will sing praise to the name of the Lord most High."*

We find here two keys to walking on faith.

Firstly when wickedness and iniquity come against us praise is the answer, and when temptation comes it soon disappears in the face of audible praise and worship. There is an old saying which goes like this;

**"The weakest saint will satan rout, who meets him with a praiseful shout"**.

There is great strength in maintaining a praiseful and

thankful heart.

Secondly, the psalmist says "I will praise the Lord". Praise is a conscious act of the will, it is not just an overflowing of exuberance but a self- induced declaration of thanksgiving, in essence a "sacrifice of praise". The person chooses in faith to praise God because He is worthy regardless of our circumstance. Remember Paul and Silas had a praise meeting in the Philippian Gaol, before the deliverance came. Two facts about praise that we must grasp are these.

- Don't wait for favourable conditions.
- Offer praise to God He is always worthy of praise and thanksgiving, and it is always the right thing to do.

*Isaiah 61:3*

*"to grant those who mourn in Zion, giving them beauty instead of ashes.*

*The oil of joy for mourning, The garment of praise for the spirit of heaviness. That they might be called trees of righteousness, the planting of the Lord that He may be Glorified"*

This is part of the scripture which Jesus read in His home town synagogue in Nazareth, a prophecy which He said was fulfilled by Him. He came therefore to set the prisoners free, but to also give us a garment of praise, to remove the spirit of heaviness. The Hebrew word *Atah* shows that praise is more than a garment thrown over our shoulder, it is a garment used to wrap or cover ourselves with completely. The garment of praise has no openings through which the enemy can get in. The garment of praise repels and replaces the heavy spirits. We must choose to put on this garment just as we choose to "put off the old man". The old man is not taken off us but is put off by us, and the garment of praise must be put on. A coat left in the wardrobe, no matter how good a coat it may be, is of no use if left on the wardrobe, for its value to be experienced it must be put on. Similarly for us to gain the benefit of what Jesus offers us we must put on praise. When distressed and depressed be dressed in a garment of praise, and act in accordance with Gods word. This is not to minimize in any way the real and awful pressure of depression, it is not saying "shake yourself it will be ok", but simply pointing the reader to the provision and promises of God, available in praise.

*Psalm 150 The* last psalm in the Book of Praises

*"Praise the Lord; Praise Him in His sanctuary. Praise Him in the mighty expanse. , Praise Him for His mighty acts. Praise Him according to His excellent greatness. Praise Him with the sound of the trumpet, praise Him with lute and harp. Praise Him with the timbrel and dance. Praise Him with the stringed instruments and flutes. Praise Him with loud cymbals Praise Him with clashing cymbals.*

*Let everything that has breath Praise the Lord.*

*Psalm 149* tells us to praise the Lord "with a new song" and to do so in the "assembly of the saints". The psalmist also specifies two outflows.

- Verse 7-9 shows it defeats the enemies that come against us.
- Verse 4 tells us the Lord takes pleasure in us and beautifies us or sanctifies us.

Paul writing to the Hebrews and speaking of Jesus gives us a profound view of worship.

*Hebrews 2:11-12*

*"For both He who sanctifies and those who are being*

*sanctified are all from one Father; for which reason He is not ashamed to call them brethren. Saying " I will declare your name to my brethren, in the midst of the congregation I will sing praise"*

This is wonderful, as Gods people worship and praise and glorify God, Jesus as our brother, the first fruits of redemption, joins with us "declaring His Father's name " His attributes , His mind and His will to us, and releasing to us severally as He wills the Gifts of the Spirit in prophesy and so on, which edifies the whole body. We read in scripture that there is joy in heaven when one sinner repents. What joy there must be when Jesus joins the singing with the redeemed glorifying God, surely all heaven must stop and listen.

Every saint of God will from time to time experience dry seasons, and the cure or antidote for these times is praise. *Numbers 21* tells us of a time when God said to Moses to gather the people so that I might give them water. God always want to water the flock, He is the good shepherd. When the got to the appointed place, verse 17 tells us Israel sang the following.

*"Spring up O well! Sing to it*

*The well which the leaders sank, which the nobles of the people dug*

*With the scepter and with the staffs"*

In times of dryness , pressure, anxiety, depression do not spend time complaining or even in analyzing the cause, start praising God for the promises He has made, start singing like Israel and starts digging and soon the water will spring up. The enemy would have you live in unbelief that the well will not produce what God has promised, but praise is the answer to that lie. Praise is the cure for all dry times, and just as Israel had water we will have water. Look at the truths in this passage.

1.    God instructs Moses gather the people. There is unity and power in corporate gatherings of Gods people. Jesus said when two or three are gathered in my name, I am there. Also if two agree about anything it will be done. Church, in whatever form, large or small, is crucial and Paul's caution not t neglect the assembling of ourselves together is more needed today than ever.

2.     God always promises, "I will give them water". God cannot lie, and in every circumstance will come through for us, and keep His promise.

3.     The people responded in obedience, by gathering, by believing. They declared faith by singing "Spring Up" Our responsibility is to worship in unity, with purpose and believing.

4.     In times of dryness, do not remain alone; gather with the praising saints, regardless of how you feel. Sing praise for past blessings and faith in His promises for now and future. The story is told of an old saint who when asked what her favourite bible verse was replied *"It came to past"* and as we praise God in our circumstance we will see it always does. Jesus in *John 4:14* declared *"whoever drinks the water that I shall give them will never thirst again, for the water I shall give will become like a fountain of water in him, springing up unto eternal life"*. We see this power of the unity of praise in *2 Chronicles 5:11-14.*

*"and it came to pass (the lady's favourite verse) when the priests came out of the Most Holy Place, (for all the priests who were present had sanctified themselves without regard to their divisions) and all*

*the Levites who were singers all those of Asaph and Heman and Jeduthan and their sons and kinsmen stood at the east end of the altar clothed in white linen, having cymbals, stringed instruments, and harps and with one hundred and twenty priests sounding trumpets. Indeed it came to pass when the trumpeters and singers were as one to make one sound to be heard in praising and thanksgiving to the Lord and when they lifted up their voices with the sound of trumpets and cymbals and instruments of music and praised the Lord saying "For He is good, for His mercy endures forever that the house of the Lord was filled with a cloud. So that the priests could not stand or continue ministering because of the cloud, for the Glory of the Lord filled the house of God".*

This is a clear demonstration of the power of unity of praise thanksgiving and music. The trumpets and the singers were as one to make one sound of praise and thanksgiving as they declared "The Lord He is good". In that they God had a physical temple, but now redeemed by the blood of Christ we are the Temples of the Spirit, so we should be offering praise and being filled with the Spirit to the Glory of God.

17

Unity and unison of such a diverse set of instruments require that all follow the same pattern of music and similarly we in corporate worship must strive to do all things decently and in order. Remember this that even in worship God is not the author of confusion. *1 Corinthians 14:23* instructs us that all things must be done decently and in order. Anything that draws attention to the worshiper and away from God, away from Jesus and the Holy Spirit ought to be avoided.

5.     At some stage read the whole story in *2 Chronicles 20* it gives us a great lesson on the power of praise. Judah was confronted by their two mortal enemies, Moab and Ammon. The people sought God in prayer and faith in His word (verse 1-14). Then came the Lord's word through the prophet;   "Do *not be afraid for the battle is not yours but God's"*. Verse 17 let them know a great truth *"You need not fight in this battle, station yourselves, stand and see the salvation of the Lord on your behalf"*. And the victory came in a strange way, but a powerful way. The Levites stood and praised the Lord God of Israel with *"very loud voices"* verse 19. Then they appointed some to sing to the Lord and some to

praise Him, *"in the beauty of His holiness"*. These all went ahead of the army singing praise to the Lord singing *"give thanks to the Lord for His loving kindness is everlasting"*. The result of this powerful praise was total and absolute victory. Praise not only brings victory it also stops the advance of wickedness. Powerful and audible praise will bring the presence of Jesus driving out all desire to identify with sinful acts, thoughts and deeds. *Psalm 47:6-7 " sing praises to God sing praises , sing praises to God sing praises for He is the King of the whole earth. Sing praises with understanding"* With understanding can also be rendered "sing all who have understanding" or "sing a skillful psalm". The Hebrew word *HebSakhl =prudent or cautious or intelligence.* When we sing praise to God with understanding or intelligence or as a conscious act of will, we are giving testimony to God's love for us and our love for Him. The result is Life instead of death. Others listening to us praising God hear testimony of our salvation and our joyful relationship with Him, which will draw them by the Holy Spirit to cry out and receive salvation for themselves. *Psalm 50, shows* us that praise is the road to a successful life. The whole psalm relates to the power and majesty and glory of God, and is summed up in the closing verses, which apply to us and Israel. If we leave God out of our lives and live in rebellion, destruction follows. In contrast the psalm sets out the simple road to success.

**a.** Offer praise and we glorify God. The focus of praise is God, but we receive wisdom and as a result are the ultimate beneficiaries.

**b.** We receive power to order our conduct thus our lifestyle comes under the control of the Spirit and therefore into obedience to God.

**c.** As our lives become ordered the revelation of our absolute salvation becomes a reality as we see our hearts and lives change.

Our praise then is a means by which God can come to us in a powerful way and minister to us and through us. *Psalm 63: 1-5* written by David when he was in the wilderness of Judah.

*"O God you are my God, early will I seek You, my soul thirsts for you. My flesh longs for You as in a dry and thirsty land where there is no water. So I looked for You in Your sanctuary, to see Your power and Your Glory. Because Your loving kindness is*

*better than life, my lip shall praise You. Thus will I bless You while I live. I will lift up my hands in Your name. My soul shall be satisfied as with marrow and fatness and my mouth shall praise you with joyful lips."*

This psalm teaches how our expressed praise releases the blessings of praise. Notice this is not s silent prayer. "My mouth shall you with joyful lips" and the fruit that flows is clear.

a. "O God You are my God": A relationship affirmed.

b. "Early will I seek You": An ordered priority

c. "My soul Thirsts My Flesh Longs": A desire for the things of God and Church Life.

d. "Because Your love is better than life my lips shall praise You": Gratitude

e. "My soul (the real me) shall be satisfied": Our provision is God.

Praise produces power as we see in *Matt 21:15-16* "But *when the chief priests and scribes saw the wonderful things that He did and the children crying out in the temple saying "Hosanna to the Son of David they were indignant. And they said to Him "do you hear what these are saying?" And Jesus said to them, "Yes Have you never read out of the mouth of babes and nursing infants You have perfected praise".* Jesus in response to the priest's objections to the praise of the people, a powerful verbal and strong praise, was to quote *Psalm 8 in* which we see that perfect praise produces strength, itself being powerful. At the very moment Jesus is being rejected by the leaders these young people are captivated by Jesus as they see Him. Catching the revelation of who He is they burst out in praise. How pleasant and heartening to Jesus this must have been as He moved toward the cross.

Praise opens prison doors. The record of Paul and Silas in *Acts 16:20-26* never ceases to encourage all who are in bondage of any kind. As we study this we have an example of the power of praise in the most difficult and trying situations. Beaten and locked in chains in a damp dungeon, Paul and Silas responded not by complaining but singing hymns of praise, songs sung directly from the heart, truly where Jesus is 'tis heaven there. The relationship between their songs of praise and their supernatural deliverance by an earthquake cannot be missed. Praise directed toward God can shale open any prison door. The jailer was converted and all his household was saved and satanic activity overthrown in

Philippi. Today as well as then praise will cause us to walk in the revelation that every chain has been broken and every prison opened. When we are serving God and things do not seem to be going as planned, learn from this text above, Praise triumphs gloriously. Again I quote "the weakest saint may satan rout who meets him with a prayerful shout".

Praise releases the Gift of Prophesy through the Holy Spirit. *Hebrews2:11-12* records this:

*"For both He who sanctifies and those who are being sanctified are one; for which reason He is not ashamed to call them brethren saying "I will declare your name to my brethren, in the midst of the assembly I will sing praise to you" Jesus* speaks declaring the Father by the Spirit in our midst. What a wonderful, the most wonderful thing about praise. Paul is quoting the messianic prophecy of *Psalm 22*, showing that the Spirit of Christ would fill the New Testament Church, and how Jesus so closely identifies with His people when they sing praises. Two important things occur when we praise.

- Jesus joins with us.

- Prophesy is released: "I will declare Your name to my brethren.

As we joyfully sing praise to our god, Jesus comes in like a flood to our minds and spirits with the glory of the Fathers character. There is no doubt as we praise in a church service, divine revelation is imparted to us by the Holy Spirit magnifying God through His son Jesus. In *Hebrews 13:15* we are exhorted;

*"Therefore by Him (Jesus) let us continually offer the sacrifice of praise to God"* That is the fruit of our lips giving thanks to God. Praise is a sacrifice. Sacrifice demands a killing, and praise requires that we kill our pride, our fears any sectarian spirit or racial prejudice, our selfishness and anything that hinders our worship and praise of the Lord. We also note here the bases of our praise, which is the sacrifice that Jesus made of Himself at Calvary. It is by Him, in Him, with Him and to Him and for Him that we offer our sacrifice of praise. Our praise is never hindered when we focus on Jesus, the author and finisher of our faith and salvation. His cross, His blood, His love and gift of life, His forgiveness, the promise that He will keep us , will keep our praise as living sacrifice to Him.

In *Genesis 29:25* we read the following:

*"and she bore a son and said. Now I will praise the Lord. Therefore she called His name Judah, meaning praise."* God chose the tribe of Judah to be the one that Jesus would be born from. Judah was not the priestly tribe that was Levi, but Paul in *Hebrews 7:12* tells us that the changing of the Law, from the Law of Moses to the Law of Liberty and Life in Jesus also required a change of the priesthood, and He tells us Jesus was after the order of Melchizdek.

*1 Peter 2: 9 tells us;*

*"But you are a chosen generation a royal priesthood, a holy nation, a people of God's own possession that you may proclaim the excellence's of Him who called you out of darkness into His marvelous light".*

Our position as those redeemed out of Adams race, translates us into the sons of the second Adam Jesus. In Him as New creations we are anointed to be priests. **Revelation 5:10:** speaking of men from every tribe and nation says.

**"And Thou hast made them to be a kingdom and priests to our God".**

The church is the chosen generation of God, Eclektos, the picked up. The word designates one gathered, one picked up  one chosen. Believers in Christ are the recipients of the favour of God, Ephesians *2:8*

*"For by Grace you are saved"*. We are Gods elect according to **Romans 8:33.** *Colossians 3:12-17* outlines for us the expectation God has for His children. *"Put on a heart of compassion, kindness humility gentleness and patience. Bear with one another and forgiving one another, whoever has a complaint against anyone, as Jesus did forgive. Beyond all these put on love which is the perfect bond of unity. Let the peace of God rule in your heart to which indeed you were called in one body and be thankful. Let the word of Christ richly dwell in you, with all wisdom, teaching and admonishing one another with Hymns and spiritual songs, singing with thankfulness in your heart to God. And whatever you do in word or deed, do all in the name of the Lord giving thanks through Him to God"*

The text of *1 Peter 2* appoints us to the ministry of praise (priests) but represents a basic revelation of scriptures to us, as to our calling. God has always wanted a people who would walk with Him in prayer, march with Him in praise thanksgiving and worship, empowered by the Holy Spirit and operating all the manifestations and gifts of the Holy Spirit. Peter describes this new covenant people.

• A Chosen generation, a people started as Jesus chose His initial twelve, who became the 120, to whom were added 3000 on the day of Pentecost, and daily afterwards, and is still being added to today, praise God.

• We are a royal priesthood. In the Old covenant the role of priest and king, or priesthood and royalty were separate. But Jesus is King of King and Lord of Lords, and our High Priest. And as we are "in Christ" we are also deemed to be priests and kings, living and reigning with Him. As a worshiping body we fight against darkness bringing His life to the world.

• We are a Holy Nation, the middle wall of partition between Jew and Greeks removed; there is neither Jew nor Greek, bond nor free, male nor female. There is no racial difference, nor rich no poor.

We are Gods peculiar people! This is what He intended from the beginning, and in His selection on Abraham, a people saved through faith by grace, to proclaim Hos praise and His majesty, His love and His blessings. We worship the King of Kings and the Lord of Lords. Praise His Holy name!

## Psalm 145:1

David's *Psalm* of praise.

I will extol thee, my God, O king; and I will bless thy name for ever and ever.
² Every day will I bless thee; and I will praise thy name for ever and ever.
³ Great *is* the LORD, and greatly to be praised; and his greatness *is* unsearchable.
⁴ One generation shall praise thy works to another, and shall declare thy mighty acts.
⁵ I will speak of the glorious honour of thy majesty, and of thy wondrous works.
⁶ And *men* shall speak of the might of thy terrible acts: and I will declare thy greatness.
⁷ They shall abundantly utter the memory of thy great goodness, and shall sing of thy righteousness.
⁸ The LORD *is* gracious, and full of compassion; slow to anger, and of great mercy.
⁹ The LORD *is* good to all: and his tender mercies *are* over all his works.
¹⁰ All thy works shall praise thee, O LORD; and thy saints shall bless thee.
¹¹ They shall speak of the glory of thy kingdom, and talk of thy power;
¹² To make known to the sons of men his mighty acts, and the glorious majesty of his kingdom.
¹³ Thy kingdom *is* an everlasting kingdom, and thy dominion *endureth* throughout all generations.
¹⁴ The LORD upholdeth all that fall, and raiseth up all *those that be* bowed down.
¹⁵ The eyes of all wait upon thee; and thou givest them their meat in due season.
¹⁶ Thou openest thine hand, and satisfiest the desire of every living thing.
¹⁷ The LORD *is* righteous in all his ways, and holy in all his works.
¹⁸ The LORD *is* nigh unto all them that call upon him, to all that call upon him in truth.
¹⁹ He will fulfil the desire of them that fear him: he also will hear their cry, and will save them.
²⁰ The LORD preserveth all them that love him: but all the wicked will he destroy.
²¹ My mouth shall speak the praise of the LORD: and let all flesh bless his holy name for ever and ever. (Ps. 145:1-21 KJV)

Printed in Great Britain
by Amazon